MW01096377

I SAW GOD
DANCING

To Joseph
Meander
in
Grace
Cheryl

The DreamSeeker
Poetry Series

Books in the DreamSeeker Poetry Series, intended to make available fine writing by Anabaptist-related poets, are published by Cascadia Publishing House under the DreamSeeker Books imprint and often copublished with Herald Press. Cascadia oversees content of these poetry collections in collaboration with DreamSeeker Poetry Series Editor Jean Janzen as well as in consultation with its Editorial Council and the authors themselves.

1. On the Cross
   By Dallas Wiebe, 2005
2. I Saw God Dancing
   By Cheryl Denise, 2005
3. Evening Chore
   By Shari Miller Wagner, 2005

Also worth noting are two poetry collections that would likely have been included in the series had it been in existence then:

1. Empty Room with Light
   By Ann Hostetler, 2002
2. A Liturgy for Stones
   By David Wright, 2003

I SAW GOD DANCING

Poems by
Cheryl Denise

(signature: Cheryl Denise)

<u>DreamSeeker Poetry Series, Volume 2</u>

DreamSeeker Books
TELFORD, PENNSYLVANIA

an imprint of
Cascadia Publishing House

Copublished with
Herald Press
Scottdale, Pennsylvania

Cascadia Publishing House orders, information, reprint permissions:
contact@CascadiaPublishingHouse.com
1-215-723-9125
126 Klingerman Road, Telford PA 18969
www.CascadiaPublishingHouse.com

I Saw God Dancing
Copyright © 2005 by Cascadia Publishing House
Telford, PA 18969
All rights reserved
DreamSeeker Books is an imprint of Cascadia Publishing House
Copublished with Herald Press, Scottdale, PA
Library of Congress Catalog Number: 2004028813
ISBN: 1-931038-28-7
Book design by Cascadia Publishing House
Cover design by Gwen M. Stamm

The paper used in this publication is recycled and meets the
minimum requirements of American National Standard for Information
Sciences—Permanence of Paper for Printed Library Materials, ANSI Z39.48-1984.1984

Grateful acknowledgement is made to the editors
of the publications where many of these poems appeared or are forthcoming.
The publications are listed on page 88 of this book.

Library of Congress Cataloguing-in-Publication Data
Denise, Cheryl, 1965-
I saw god dancing : poems / by Cheryl Denise.
   p. cm. -- (DreamSeeker poetry series ; v. 2)
ISBN 1-931038-28-7 (trade pbk. : alk. paper)
   1. Mennonites--Poetry. 2. West Virginia--Poetry. 3. Ontario--Poetry. I. Title.
II. Series.
PS3604.E585I17 2005
811'.6--dc22

                                                              2004028813

12 11 10 09 08 07 06 05   10 9 8 7 6 5 4 3 2 1

Thanks to Lori Oesch for belief,
Barbara Smith for know-how,
and Sandy Vrana for wisdom

Contents

Someone Like You

✿

Before the Service

He meanders in grace,
eyes wrinkling into his cheeks,
lips mingling with the divine,
arms reaching heaven.
He hushes sin in a breath,
his hands stained with prayer.
I sit in the back
listening to him prepare.
Silence entwined with names,
Michael . . . Darla . . . Julie.
I wait for mine
feeling it slide through his mouth,
mysteriously rising
like incense toward God. ✤

Grace

Mennonites don't dance.
It's not something you ask about:
mothers sour, fling their hands,
squawk frenzied sermons.
I used to sneak downstairs in the dark,
turn on the TV and join
the National Ballet of Canada.

When I was eleven,
my legs grown long,
I asked Dad for Nutcracker tickets.
I think he was happy,
my first time at a city stage
not filled with a choir.

I wanted to dance, to pirouette,
a Mary Magdalene spilling her perfume. ❧

Mennonite Poet

Dedication

We begin life crying in front of a congregation,
in a circle of parents
with dark suits and crisp, clean dresses,
grandparents near the front
who wish we'd hush.
The pastor touches our foreheads
with rough farm hands,
asks our parents to nurture us in Christ;
the congregation in semi-unison promises to help.
Five minutes and it's done
we're taken back to our seats
sucking our mothers' fingers,
immersed in the thunderous four-part harmony
of "Children of the Heavenly Father."

Our Father

At four we're taught to pray
in Sunday school rooms filled with pictures
of David and sling shots,
long-haired Samson breaking down pillars,
white-bearded Noah laughing,
guiding giraffes into the Ark.
We fold our hands,
bow our heads;
"Our Father," we awkwardly mumble,
cheeks filled with crackers.
Kneeling, we're told, is good,
but only in private.

I spied on Mom and Dad
but never caught them at it.

Sunday Dinners

At ten I am expected to lead my younger sisters
in helping with Sunday dinners and company.
Our table was always full,
we girls sitting at the corners
ready to refill plates of roast beef and potatoes.

We laugh as three men
rub their rough-trimmed beards and tell stories,
how they left the Old Order Church at eighteen,
no more farming or horse and buggies.
They met secretly one night at the corner of
Eli's meadow and walked to the city.
Naive, in suspenders and work boots,
they crossed on red.
A policeman gave them a ten-dollar ticket.

Dessert lasts till three
apple pies with Crisco crusts
slices of sharp cheddar on top.
We serve mint tea
and offer seconds,
have to stay seated and listen
to the last scrap of adult conversation.
From the living room window
we can see the neighbor kids
picking teams for soccer.

After Church

At sixteen I hang around after everyone leaves
and write to the hum of Roy's vacuum downstairs.
I wonder about sharing a poem
for Kendal's baptism.
Poetry, like my first time on skates,
is still awkward and exciting.
I envy Catholic poets,
gold statues, holy water,
stained glass colors of salvation.
All I see is a smooth pine cross
hanging in this jaundiced sanctuary,
where it just seems prudent to believe. ❧

Quilt Makers

I sit with Grandma
in a circle of women,
warm with belonging.
She jokes in Pennsylvania Dutch
while fingers long and calloused
quilt pieces of family—
Uncle Joe's work shirts,
Aunt Edna's baby clothes,
Mother's high school dresses,
piecing everything from polyester
to cotton,
to lay on marriage beds,
soften cradles,
warm children in winter.
She learned from her mother, her grandmother,
her great-grandmother in Weinsburg.
Someday she'll fit my sister's thumb
with a thimble, too,
when she's too big to play dolls
under the quilt frame.
We all will sit on Saturday afternoons,
ready. ✤

Communion

Patsy, my best friend, was Catholic.
They had communion every Sunday;
she thought four times a year wasn't enough.
From a gold goblet they drank wine;
the Priest made it into the actual blood.
We drank Welch's Grape Juice
from tiny plastic cups,
and washed feet.
The women were dismissed to the basement;
Mom said they kept their stockings on.
The men went up front in pairs.
We kids stood on the pews,
watching them kneel
holding each other's feet over basins,
pouring water from heavy white pitchers
then rubbing with thin white towels.
Afterwards they kissed each other,
the only time I ever saw them hug;
Dad said it was holy. ❧

Kissing Tag

Grade two at recess I ran fast,
except once
when Fish caught me at the garbage bins.
I thought for a second he wouldn't do it,
fixing me with his eyes, holding me against green metal
before quickly banging his face into mine.

That afternoon he waited by the stoplights,
looked at me for a nod or something,
grabbed my hand.
For three days, forever it seemed, we walked in silence a half-
mile to the end of my drive.

I heard Mom tell Aunt Lucy in the kitchen, I had a boyfriend.
It was nine o'clock and I was supposed to be asleep
and knew enough not to defend myself.

Fish was pale and blonde,
his hair long in the back like a teenager's.
He didn't go to church and he swore some.
With the boys he talked kind of funny, fast
like he'd been to the jungle and was going back.

Then one afternoon he just wasn't there.
He must have grown bored
and I was relieved.

We've never spoken
even all through high school.
After graduation I moved to the Rockies,
he stayed in Elmira, a job at the feed mill.

Fifteen years since I've thought of him,
then yesterday my sister sends me the *Woolwich Observer*
and there he is in black and white his hair blown in the night wind,
leaning outside the Steddick, the only place in town
Mom told me never to go.
A beer and a cigarette, an easy smile,
township goes smoke free
but not Fish,
staring at me
to come home and taste the wild. ❦

These Visions

It's 3 a.m.
my coffee and the Milky Way
lingering,
I almost hear you ask,
"Are you sleeping?"
I wish I could
sneak to your room,
feel the stories,
your first date with Paul,
how Brian asked me out,
your plans to quit at Shop Easy.

I told a story in church today,
how you once reminded me of Jesus.
You said you'd take the blame
for the iron I broke.

I remember sitting beside you
at Dad's baseball games,
sharing that red-checkered blanket,
collecting pop bottles,
buying gum balls,
red licorice,
missing home runs
while we talked.

Now I can't sleep
trying to read Steinbeck
his words and Grandma's quilt blurring
wondering if you're thinking about me. ✤

While Sitting On My Porch Steps
I think of you
at the kitchen table with my mother
eating butter tarts,
while I put on one more coat
of mascara.

Clean cropped hair,
football shoulders,
Russian Mennonite voice.

I wondered why you had to sit next to me,
at the theater.
I felt sick.
And you asked,
listened
while I told you
about the guy in a shaker knit sweater
grabbing my breasts
at 6 a.m. on King St.
waiting for the light to change,
his tongue in and out of my ear.
You said we could forgo dances,
holding hands;
we could walk with spaces between us.
You called the next morning.

Saturdays you taught me to swing a bat
stout and sure
as an Old Order girl.
We practiced catching

fly balls, grounders,
getting ready for Sunday afternoons
with the youth group from church.

I remember riding home
on the back of your Harley,
that maroon Chevy veering in front of us
in the dark rain
so close to our thighs.

You said you loved me once.
I wanted the readiness for old age,
suppers at KFC.
I hadn't left yet for college.
I didn't know
in the white walls of your room
listening to Rush
that it was my last chance to say it,
and not feel cheap
like it was just about
being nineteen and new.
I didn't know our next good-bye embrace
would be awkward
and then I'd never see you again. ❧

Missing Someone Like You
Saturday nights I tagged along
on your dates with Becca.
At the gallery she shared the stories
of her big-hipped women
in charcoal and water colors.

I liked the way you smiled,
your hair the dusty color of tumbleweed,
your talk of cattle and coyotes.

Becca taught me to two-step
on our kitchen floor
Sundays after church.
We laughed at the static
on the radio,
dancing until we were
too hungry for lunch.

You were shy
and while you waited for her,
you danced quiet with me.
I felt safe in your arms
knowing your hands would not
slide down the straights of my hips.
You stopped only for quick kisses from her,
hors d'oeuvres we couldn't pronounce,
boxed wine.

The next morning Becca made me eggs
with salsa and sharp cheddar

and told me how you and she went star-gazing
after I went to bed.

You, rooted in this valley
looking for a wife, a mother for your six-year-old.
She asked me if she should break it off.
I convinced her to stay. ❖

My People

My people are quiet
and don't always say
what they want
what they need.
They leave things off
for you to figure out.

They read Bibles and think a lot
but would never tell you their thoughts
unless asked,
and even then
they would speak quietly
with a slow strong sense
of who God is.
They ask what you believe
and listen.

My people say they don't make oatmeal rolls
as good as Grandma's;
even Grandma says this.
My people make carrot juice
and like it.
My Grandpa, who's blind,
can play pool
and beat you.

We eat at long fancy tables
with cloth napkins
and say grace before meals.
Mom makes pumpkin soup

with a little—a little more—
maple syrup.

Creamy chocolates,
raspberry truffles, hazelnut creams;
my people know real love.

My people love to feed church visitors,
Mrs. Brubacher in the nursing home,
even their gay neighbor.
Everyone needs food,
good food
from Sittler's Bakery in Conestogo,
the Old Order women in the kitchen
rolling sweet dough,
bosoms cloudy with flour.

My people think the only sin
God really doesn't care about
is gluttony, a second piece of pie.

My people drink
fresh squeezed orange juice
in the morning,
use half-and-half,
always have four different kinds of bread
in their kitchens.

They talk of things they don't agree with
or understand—
liberals, Catholics, ultraconservatives,

the Daves, blacks,
but when they meet one
they offer shoo-fly pie
and a coffee,
a little conversation,
and afterwards they'll say,
Well, that one was okay.

My people don't understand your people,
but we'll feed you. ✤

Motherhood

(for Karah)

I have something to say to you
and the baby
kicking at your once flat belly,
to tell you
this thing you're doing,
planned out and loved:
this disturbance to everything
normal and calm
is beautiful.

Soon you'll forget to polish your nails,
you'll cut your hair short,
never have time for a Saturday novel
or the luxury of bathroom reading.

You'll feel fogged over,
reduced to
a wisp of a person
anything could blow over.

I want to warn you
that coffee and chocolate,
onions and sauerkraut,
Pepsi and pizza
don't go well with breast milk,

that a girl in my office last week
asked what can be done
for stretch marks.
There was no answer.

You won't listen to Madonna
anymore.
You'll pay attention to the words
on your CDs
and be appalled.

You'll start watching PBS,
scan for appropriate programming
still bearable to adults.

No more suppers in front of the TV,
you'll plan nutritious meals
around the table,
the kitchen counter now full of bottles
and soft plastic nipples.

You'll be up at 2 a.m.
and forget how to sleep,
really sleep,
that I-don't-exist-for-anyone
kind of sleep.

In sweatpants you'll crunch sit-ups
on the living room floor,
not caring who walks in,
thinking you don't look gorgeous
when you do.

You'll spill stories of labor,
broken water, contractions,
positions, longed-for drugs.
You'll brag how long it took,
tell how horrible or wonderful your husband was.

Soon you'll forget
what used to make you happy,
what you thought everything was about.

You'll buy how-to books for new parents,
listen to advice by mothers in the Henning's parking lot.
You'll practice everything you learned from your mother
from baking funny cakes and shoo-fly pies,
to making conversation and laughter
feel like soft hymns.

One Sunday morning
you'll be sitting in church
with a beautiful baby
wrapped in whispers,
sleeping through prayers, invocations,
the very message of God,
which he already knows. ❧

Sister

I couldn't finish reading
Emily Brontë's "Stars";
I was thinking of you.

I remember your last visit,
a thin, watery three-day weekend.
I was so busy finishing your quilt.

Sometimes I want to leave this life
and run away to yours,
but I can't.
I've become like our old neighbor Mrs. Kaufmann
(the one we always made fun of),
who wears her hair too grey,
too down,
pulls on old coats from thrift stores,
laughs at people who can't can
their own tomatoes,
her greatest pleasure darning socks.

I've always lived somewhere
with too many teenagers for you.
So how have you been and all that?
As if you'd tell me in a letter.

I need you
like old shoes and orange juice.
I wish it were yesterday
and we were twelve,
making plans to marry brothers,
riding white horses all afternoon. ❧

My Name is Ruth

I've got seventeen cats;
Isabella's my favorite,
and Patty doesn't mind,
thin and doing dishes
three times a week.
She gets paid by the Center.
I have no doors inside,
pink flowered curtains instead,
made them myself.

Mr. Larson doesn't like my house—
peeling paint,
holes in the windows.
He wants a respectable town,
neat homes
with ceramic lawn ornaments.
He's trying to get me to move
to the Senior Apartments.
He'd burn this place down himself
if he wasn't the mayor.

The town never much cared for me—
Dad always drunk and scared in the streets.
Mom lied to get WIC,
used food stamps to buy cigarettes.
They're dead now
and I have my own TV,
thirty-two channels
if you hook them wires up just right.

The neighbor boys steal my tomatoes,
throw them against the gate
but that doesn't bother me—
I like splotches of red
on white paint.

Friday mornings the health nurse comes over
stinking of Ivory soap and shampooed hair,
enough to make a fit of coughing.
She said my toenails were too long
and made Patty soak them for a week
before she'd come back and cut them.

I've written two novels,
five books of poetry,
got them sitting on my nightstand.
Nobody'll read them.
Heard Mrs. Higginbacher wrote another book.
She's at the library now
painted up, signing autographs.
She failed me in fourth grade,
only the pretty girls got A's.
I know a lot more about writing
than she does.
Last night I wrote a children's story,
rhymed.

I wear a rosary I found on the street
by the Post Office.
They said I stole it
from little Suzy.

No use to give it back,
her mamma told her not to talk to me,
wouldn't want to scare the kid.

Rev. Johnson stops by after church,
brings cat food.
His parishioners won't drink
Christ's blood from the same cup as me,
so I don't go.

I'll be dead soon.
They'll torch this place
before my body cools,
by then I'll be laughing, flying over this town,
silver hair glowing forever.
Me in a coffee stained orange robe
with wings. ✿

Eddie's Laundromat

I watch
snickering women in pink sponge curlers,
wrinkled women with cigarettes and grandsons,
tight women, made up like Cosmopolitan covers,
heave black garbage bags
of church dresses, pink baby outfits,
and sweaty smelly work pants
onto sticky countertops.
K-Mart pictures
of generic apple trees
and rich farmyards
hang crooked overhead.

I press the delicate cycle
while dreaming of
setting quarters in the slots
of your machines,
of asking the names of your grandsons,
of buying you Cokes,
of laughing under your warm brown eyes.

Instead, I settle into a cracked
green plastic chair
and finger year old *Good Housekeepings*,
while you talk of layoffs,
and late husbands,
Tommy's wreck on 76,
and Joetta's coal fire.
You stop to tell me my washer's quit
and point me to one of the few hot dryers.

I stumble a thank-you
while gathering my load,
as you return to stories:
dry crops, and miscarriages,
broken red tractors. ❖

God and Farmers

I'm not sure
but I think God likes farmers best,
people that work outside in blue jeans.

I don't get it,
why they're so poor,
unless God wants them
to have the very best of heaven.

I bet He doesn't watch us much
in offices
over spreadsheets and lawyer briefs,
He gets bored.

Mom said when the bridge on 21 went out,
the one the horse and buggies use,
the township proposed a hundred thousand dollar plan
to be completed in six months.
The Old Orders decided to do it themselves,
in a week it was done
for twenty-five.

Farmers know how God made the earth.
When something dies they make something else live.
Their bodies last longer.
They don't need gyms, spandex, magazine diets.

Farmers get that noontime famished feeling
not the dull rumblings after inside work.
They know where food comes from;
they pray better.

It's easy to forget God in offices.
I can't see God calling someone to be a financial planner.
Even jobs we think of as good
get all screwed up.

Nursing seems noble, working with old people
but sometimes I think
if I just let the residents go outside more,
bring in golden Labs and chickadees,
stop giving out pills,
God and the old folks would hold hands more.

It's easy to like lobster in the city,
to go to Pittsburgh to see the ballet,
to have nice homes in pretty neighborhoods
to keep the kids safe,
but I don't know that God wants our money
if we're rich.

I think in heaven
God will tell the farmers jokes
the rest of us won't understand.
I think they'll still farm
because they want to,
but if a crop goes bad,
God will order them pizza and beer.
At noon when the angels harp
and the rest of us sing,
God and the farmers will be playing games,
making the corn and wheat sway. ✤

Our Jacob Sheep

People always ask,
they know your voice;
they follow you?

I am not Jesus
and these sheep follow
an old drywall bucket with feed
that I shake
while yelling, *Eh Woolly Woolly,*
hoping they'll follow me.

They ignore me
then one by one stare
stark-faced at the pail
until some ewe baas,
runs.

Dennis and Mike herd from behind,
sprawled arms waving the way.

They chase me
out the gate
past the pines
down the hill
a sharp left
into their new pasture,
feed jostles,
ewes bawl,
as if I won't feed the last ones in.

Not all of them come.
I yell louder,
violently shake the bucket.
Suddenly the rest bolt in,
Mike behind them.

I pour feed in wooden troughs,
burly wool bodies press against my legs.
Dennis closes the gate,
sighs.

Jesus must have been talking about
some different breed,
ours are biblical but old testament.
After we've led them to greener pastures
they crowd in the corner
stressed and shuffling,
like teenagers their first day back at school.

I never much liked their namesake,
Jacob,
that soft skinned mama's boy
stealing Esau's birthright.
Maybe the sheep sense it.

No, I tell anyone who asks,
our sheep are not what Jesus had in mind,
but maybe more like us. ✾

Legs

I remember Randy in math
watching my legs,
wishing his legs
were wrapped around mine.

I remember jogging through lunch hours
with other legs,
by the end of the year
my legs did more miles
than any other girl's.

Scarred above the left knee
from a Colorado hike,
climbing rocks to a hidden waterfall,
lying to Mike, telling him
just a scratch.

I love my legs in your jeans,
taking lazy muddy walks,
sleeping in patches of sunlight
next to your legs,
dancing on Sunday afternoons
to your old Bruce Cockburn tapes.

When I know you have to leave,
I put on my black leather mini skirt
with bare legs
and perfumed lotions
and you stay
a little longer.

My legs always have liked your legs,
crouched down in gardens
planting Silver Queen,
driving down dusty barren roads,
standing in old brown work boots.

I like the way my legs feel
after a shower
when you fill your hands with thoughts
and rub upwards.

My legs are happiest with your legs,
doing anything, doing nothing,
lying leg over leg over leg
in bed with you. ✤

White Oak Park

Soaking in love
like we're some modern Adam and Eve
God decided to give another garden,
we dive into this river,
the hillside crowded
with open magnolias,
green scents drenching the air.
Caught in cool, dizzying circles,
we gasp for breath.
White foam floats round my elbows
while the distant noise of average people
drifts away.
They won't climb down
and discover this forbidden passion
married people aren't supposed to have,
and I remember my old English prof
saying sex is the closest
we ever get to God.

Emerald water seeps into
all my hidden places
around our entangled legs,
your long brown hair loose
hands swimming over me.

Downstream we clamber onto
a smooth grey rock
to sun dry.

At dusk finding our stump
of heaped clothes,
we follow the path back
believing ourselves
the two most beautiful people
anywhere. ❧

I would let you in
if I knew who you were
if you'd slip into my soul
two-step with me
and Lyle Lovett
on the porch

if we could have sex
in the living room
the sun streaming in
a Wednesday afternoon

if you'd say you loved me
and always had
and it wouldn't sound like a lie

eventually we'd eat bruschetta
drink rye and Coke
smoke Players outside in the grass
watching what the night does ✿

Baby Sister

I can see you in games of hide-and-seek,
in Dessler's weeping willow,
on bicycles fast down gravel roads.
I suppose there were times
I didn't let you play with my Barbies
or listen to my Captain and Tennille records.

You were always the one
with baseball games, bruises, soccer practice,
sleeping with a giant polar bear.

The last time you were here
I gave you a children's book to read.
It's how I want you.

And if we lived together
and I was 70 and you 66
I'd still think you shouldn't cut the tomatoes
with such a big knife.

Younger sisters should grow up in shadows
that feel cool and round,
wild and safe,
and God's supposed to be better to them.

As you tell me the story over the phone,
my head drops between my knees
and I wish I were there making you hot cider
and cinnamon toast,
telling you not to go to work in the morning.

Even though I'm quite sure
your husband kissed you today,
I wish it was my kiss on your cheek.

When you say, "I must sound crazy,"
I want to tell you
about the man who called
saying grab, kiss, rape
just to let you know
how I paced the cabin so loud,
how for days I hung up on any man who called,
that I too felt strange and lost.
But I'm the oldest;
afraid if you knew,
I'd be less solid.

And already you live too far away
and open doors and packages,
nightmares and dreams
without me.

But if I could have been the one
to find the woman lying there wrong,
cold with dead eyes,
I would have breathed, instead of you,
and pushed on her heart,
and told you to go
back to Frey's sandbox
to build castles and pies. ❧

Waiting

Sheep roam the field
till bells ring
and black-eyed Susans fall
petal by petal,
and I wait.
The moon wanes
like old memories
I can't grasp anymore but feel.

You won't come.

Thoughts fall heavy as pears,
bruising.
I don't eat them
till they sour.
Crumbs of childhood
strewn at my feet are
eaten by black ants.
My head rests on a rock;
I watch downcast sunflowers,
and I forget how to make new dreams.

Tomorrow I'll plant corn
which the deer will steal.
Dirt will grow under my nails
and deepen the cracks in my hands.

At times I almost feel you again
in the wild wind.
Hope breathes against my neck
and this is enough. ❦

Sleeping Alone

❧

Mother God

Mother God, come
rock me to sleep,
read me the story
of your giving birth.
Feed me oatmeal cookies
baked by wrinkled hands.
Soothe me with
honey-laced milk.
Fold me over
in a ragged
thick quilt.
Hold my head
to your breast.
Show me the pictures
till my eyes tire
and into dreams
dance the Seven Sisters.
Kiss me then
without my knowing.
Come, Mother God,
put me to bed. ✤

Gifts

My father works to the
rhythmic clank and snort of the Heidelberg Press.
The shop used to be a chicken barn
now full of antique typewriters,
boxy Underwoods and Smith-Coronas,
the west wall stacked with trays of hand-set type.
On the counter Grandpa's black cash register sits
waiting to ring.

Dad eats an orange at ten,
an apple at three.

On my way to Shannon's
I stop at Freiburgers,
pick up and set down
a dozen Red Delicious.
I find the perfect one,
eighty-four cents,
to put on the top of Dad's mail.

At supper he gives me two tickets
to a concert
on a floating stage
at the Elora Gorge.
I take Darlene.
We listen until midnight,
pretend all the way home
we're Irish folk stars.

In bed, I think about God,
full of things to make me happy,
like barn swallows and heaven,
how I offer God such things
as eighty-four-cent apples.
He eats the gift,
juice running down his chin,
while he gives me
choirs crowded with angels. ❀

Heaven and Things

Sometimes I'm afraid to think about God,
sitting in tight pews,
squashed with girls in pretty dresses,
boys in clean blue jeans.
A round suited man paces;
faster, higher his arms raise,
his hands curl in tight fat fists.
"Wide is the path that leads to hell,"
his voice booms on long after his mouth shuts.
He unveils the felt board,
grotesque men, women on their knees,
jaws gaped open, limbs burning.
"But you can be saved, repent of your sins
and Je-Sus will wash you white as snow!"

I want to like Jesus.
He told his grouchy disciples
to let children come to him.
He held them in his lap,
said grown-ups should be more like kids.
But the picture of heaven
has girls in white gloves and frilled skirts
holding their brothers' hands,
mom and dad walking in front
on winding gold streets.
No parks, No baseball diamonds,
No candy stores.

Boredom seems better than burning,
so I keep going to church with Katie

Wednesday nights.
Sometimes we make gingerbread cookies in crosses,
thin haired women with tight grey buns
laugh over us and give mushy kisses.

But mostly Rev. Simmons yells too long,
like he has twenty cups of coffee
and the wrath of God inside him.
He tells us to bring other kids, neighbor kids,
girls we ride the bus with,
boys that shovel our mothers' drives;
in doing so we are leading others to heaven.

I don't want to lead anyone there.
Figure if they're good
and don't know about salvation
maybe God will exempt them,
and they won't have to go anywhere
after they die.
So I'm teaching my younger sister to say
please and thank-you,
telling Billie about the importance
of saying you're sorry.

I wish heaven were like Mrs. Frey's home,
stuffed with children,
filled with the smell of whoopie pies,
tall cold glasses of milk,
camp songs,
games of hide-and-seek.

I hope the angels are like
her son Michael playing jokes with eggs,
and Wanda whispering secrets.

I want God to be like Mrs. Frey
holding you in her aproned lap,
singing till you fall asleep. ❧

They'll
take your soul
and put it in a suit,
fit you in boxes
under labels,
make you look like the Joneses.

They'll tell you go a little blonder,
suggest sky-blue
tinted contact lenses,
conceal that birthmark
under your chin.

They'll urge you to have babies
get fulfilled.
They'll say marriage is easy,
flowers from Thornhills
are all you need
to keep it together.

They'll push you to go ahead,
borrow a few more grand,
build a dream house.
Your boys need Nikes,
your girls cheerleading,
and all you need is your job
9 to 5 in the same place.

They'll order you never to cry
in Southern States,
and never, ever dance
in the rain.

They'll repeat all the things
your preschool teacher said
in that squeaky too tight voice.

And when you slowly
let them go,
crack your suit,
ooze your soul
in the sun,
when you run through
the woods with your dog,
read poems to swaying cornfields,
pray in tall red oaks,
they'll whisper
and pretend you're crazy. ❀

Sleeping Alone

A printed gown once blue
pretends to hide
my wrinkled, lapped up breasts.
Stilled in the corner, the curtains
watch as I'm repositioned.
It's time.
The note at the head
of my bed says so.
While they turn me,
the sheets fall away from
the yellowing skin of my thighs.
George, my roommate's husband,
stares at something on the wall,
curses his health, reviews long talks with his son.

We're residents now, not patients.
Someone in a suit, who can wipe himself,
thought of that.

I used to wear Victorian lace,
put wild pink roses in my hair,
kiss my husband's beard.

I want my camisole,
folded once,
in the second drawer of my nightstand,
smelling of lavender.
I want candles
and wine with dinner.
I want to dance
under the sassafras tree.

Tom walks in,
it must be six,
he rubs my hands,
reads me a Silverstein poem,
smiles at me.
He used to sneak kisses
when the children weren't looking.
The children are always looking now,
spooning me white pills,
draining my urine bag,
mumbling in the hall
about how difficult I am.

Tom leaves
as my roommate's feeding tube
starts beeping.
I try to turn to watch him.
I listen for the sound of the Chevy.
I reach my hand to the other side
of my pillow. . . . ❧

Martha's Story

They told me you were coming.
I washed grandma's purple bowls,
baked oatmeal rolls in knots and crescents,
pulled out Aunt Carol's scribbled notes
for sweet potato bake,
picked dates,
cooked them into pudding,
like a wise old woman.
I dusted the walls,
washed the sheets from the guest room,
dried them in the cool November air,
set out boxes of apple and peppermint tea.
I got Jacob down the street
to kill Bessie,
his fattest chicken.

I greeted you with a kiss,
filled everyone's wine,
offered seconds, sometimes thirds.
You didn't eat much,
talking and laughing.
And Mary,
just sitting there at your feet,
like you were some kind of Messiah
made just for looking at.
And you praised her.

It's 2 a.m.
Mary's sleeping on the couch,
too full of thoughts
to help with sweeping.

Someone'll hear this story,
people are always telling stories about Jesus.
They'll say I'm a fool,
but someone had to set the table,
steep the tea,
and clean the rugs. ❧

Driving Home Alone

My foot floors the curves,
my hand smoothes the folds of my dress,
the old familiar longing to feel
the swell of your child.
Your image dark, beautiful,
in the face of every brazen trucker,
in crowded five-star restaurants,
in theaters sticky with the smell of butter.
Through every town
my mind wanders—
you making love to a stranger.

In the back of my desk drawer
you lie bare chested in the sun,
daring anyone not to let you in.
I dried your graduation roses,
but five years
of being hung, bumped, dusted,
there was nothing much to throw away.

I want the feel of you
to slide down me
sudden, forever
like you could drop from the stars,
or saunter out of the woods,
or be standing at the side of the road
waiting for my ride. ❧

Baking Bread

When the news comes,
her wedding band
is covered with dough.

While the phone receiver dangles,
she greases the pans
and rolls crescents.
She imagines
him coming home,
a smile edges his face.
The smell of bread fills the house.
His calloused hands
break a roll.
Thick the butter,
thin the elderberry jam,
he tears a piece,
drops it on her tongue.
A kiss melts her cheek.

While the bread blackens in the oven,
she can hear her sister
knocking at the door
calling her name
the day he comes back no more. ✿

God

She sways the fields
with whispers,
caresses your prayers,
as her arms reach down
through the trees.

She will cry when you mourn,
kiss your scars
with aloe lips,
soak your chest
in pools of perfume.

When you are tired
and think you can no longer
live for her,
she will rub your arms, shoulders,
like she is making new bread.

You who work for justice
will see children
red, black and pale
naked and chaste
in thick gardens
bordered with grape vines
and emerald rivers.

And you the poor,
in heaven, she will dress
in long red strips of silk
and let the whippoorwills teach you to fly,
draping the world in evening sunsets.

And you without good mothers or fathers,
she will someday
gather on her back,
let you run and hide in her
long soft hair.

She will tell you the peacemakers
ride elephants, eat mangos,
rest on the very peaks of paradise.

Someday you the meek and merciful
will see her face
etched with laughter,
her strong arms wrapped in woven blankets,
legs covered in printed skirts
from braided women in Zaire.

She will take your hands
in her big gardenia scented palms
and swing you through
ten thousand dizzying dances.
Then she will rest you
beneath bedtime stories,
till you want to dance again. ✤

Bathsheba

I think about Uriah
rugged, divinely loyal,
as I amble face forward
smiling in the marketplace.
At night he is gentle.
We laugh over wine,
he rubs my side,
I his little ewe lamb.

Alone, I bathe in
open courtyard,
spilling tiny drops of milk.
The sun plays with me,
just the two of us
until a messenger comes
declaring I must go to the King.
Awed, I wonder.

At the palace
I bow before him.
He offers me figs,
throws lavish words
while his brown eyes
then hands
ooze down my breasts.

Bed is sudden, cold,
covered in emerald quilts
with gold thread,
the sounds of servants' feet
through the walls.

Before daylight creeps
he orders me gone.

I leave his fat
marbled pillars
to wash clay pots,
bake bread without sugar;
his scent stains my home.

Late summer the sun rises full;
David's baby kicks my belly.
The neighbor women whisper
Uriah's dead,
a black shroud
rounds me
—my baby.

Gossip howls
like wind
depetaling flowers.
I go to David,
child withered inside me
    By God!
The King eats when the baby dies.
I cry.
"There, there,
Bathsheba," he says.
"You shall have another,
    come."
I see the lines of his eyes
smiling like a serpent.

I go with him. . . . ❧

Jagged Dreams

A rock flies through the kitchen window.
  I lie sleeping,
the crib slowly stops its rocking.
Rapunzel lies open
on the hardwood floor
waiting for tomorrow,
  for the prince.

Broken glass scatters on the tile.
  I lie dreaming
of an old magnolia tree,
my teacup sits on the nightstand
  stained and happy
with a half eaten Oreo beside.

The stone lands on the floor
  next to the oven
made for baking chocolate cakes
and peanut butter cookies.
Into my room gleams moonlight
dancing on the diamond shapes
  of my quilt
reaching to the crib, caressing Joleen.

The arm that threw the rock
   aches and
walks away, afraid,
to an old Ford pickup
with empty Buds
and faded pictures
of a family smiling.

I wake alone
hearing the noise
delayed in my head,
going to the kitchen
to cry in a heap
of see-through brokenness,
trying vaguely to put it away. ✤

Men

In castles live
armored men
wine-sipping men
refined men

In caves wander
meaty men
hairy-chested men
tough-jawed men

In my mind live
sweet men
suited men
kiss-your-hand men

On hillsides live
simple men
planting men
prayerful men

But I wake to you
whiskey-man
loud tempered man
fisted man ❀

Mumblings

Oozing
through the walls
cackles crackles
accusations assassinations
thump bang bump
Did I hear my name
   I sit
restlessly rocking
clamoring climbing
over things I've done
I've didn't
their words crawl
through the walls
   indistinct
they touch
sniff and snag
pecking and pulling
my rusty red hair
they taunt at my cheeks
and tear at my lashes
   I keep
recklessly rocking
concealing my senses
with radio rumblings
but they keep talking and talking ✿

At Church

While singing "Children of the Heavenly Father"
I hear your distinct tenor voice.
I remember baby-sitting your children
when I was fifteen,
sitting in the dark glow of the TV,
your boys asleep under race-car blankets,
popcorn gone,
the fridge emptied of the last piece of shoo-fly,
my eyes shocked at the
brown bottles of beer in the back.
It was then that I found them,
under the Sears Catalogue.
Shiny naked women.

After five minutes
the slow sweat of my hands
turned pages
to arched brows
and pink cheeks.
I followed the curve of hair down shoulders
over mountainous breasts,
deep valley middles
pulling into tiny buttons,
sliding down round hips,
legs slightly parted.
They lay on white couches,
kitchen floors,
in sunken bathtubs
touching themselves
like they were too beautiful to resist.

I pictured you in bed with Janice,
eyes closed imagining July's favorite.
Janice, a Barbie Doll figure
who played fast pitch for church league.
She said you remembered me
riding my tricycle to church,
blonde ribboned pig-tails,
in a blue dress.

In the bathroom closet
behind the plush white towels
stood a poster,
a brown haired woman
lying on the beach,
breasts strewn in the sun,
sand glistening on her thighs,
ready to kiss you.

I wondered how many
Mennonite men had her in the closet.

At two a.m.
naked in my bedroom,
I stared in the mirror,
imagining my future husband,
his eyes dropping away
disappointed.

Even now, years later,
I'm still afraid
to get seated beside you in the pew,

to be bumped by your arm
taking coats off in the foyer,
watching your green eyes
tear open my dress,
laughing at my apricot breasts
grabbing them anyway. ❧

God
(according to Pastor Smucker)

likes pretty women
in floral skirts
and a glory of long blonde curls.

On a Sunday afternoon,
the smell of a roast in the oven
reassures God and man
that everything is in order.

God shines his face upon women
with soft pink bibles
who go to women's groups,
talk marriage and children,
play piano,
sew bandages
to send overseas.

He likes Maybelline women
who make Jello salads
for carry-ins.

God is happiest when we're pregnant,
as long as we remember
the seed is our husband's,
and there's no correlation
between creation and birthing.

God sends men when we weep,
to stroke our foreheads
and kiss our hair.
He needs men to feel strong.

God prefers us skinny
in fancy dresses
with matching accessories;
we are his temple

God wants us silent
in business meetings,
offering lemon squares
and soothing herbal teas.

God likes our breasts
pointing heavenwards
as we pray
and do the dishes. ✸

The Manuscript

In a room without windows
I lie naked and still
on the table
surrounded by men
in plush black chairs

they speak
but not of me for hours it seems
then turning their thoughts
read the rise and fall of my body

a cigar scented man
leans forward
slowly inserts his finger
in the fat dimple on my right hip
rolls it round
takes it back

the man who brought me here
sits at my head
I can hear his thoughts
he cannot save me from this

they cut
temple to temple
greedy hands lift
whatever they want

they say words like
primitive

fresh
rhythmic

a knife slices
the bottom of my sternum
stops at my navel
there is no blood
just hands
pulling out all the images I take in
but refuse to digest

I can hear their hands
twisting and wringing

I am afraid
they won't put it back in

their words thick and mumbled
heavy
above me
as they lean back in their chairs
all easy in their suited bodies
high conversation
the scent of well cleaned skin
trimmed toenails

and they will decide ❧

The Ladies at the Reading
In the front row
the three of them giggled,
and tapped each other's knees
with wrinkled perfumed hands.
Their eyes eased over my face;
they wrapped my words 'round them.
Slight tears they tried to stop
when I read of sleeping alone.
Parting Pink Passion
and fluorescent red lips,
I heard them whisper
through the thin clapping,
"Mildred, isn't she wonderful!"
With knee high nylons crossed
and too thin-heeled shoes,
they kept my rhythm.
Their dresses sparkled silver
under oversized chandeliers;
their breasts hung pendulous
on full bellies
that sighed when I read "Bathsheba."

I should have liked to kiss them,
tasting their powdered cheeks.
I should have invited them
to drink Chablis
after the evening ended.
I would have told them my childhood,
the dreams I let escape.
I would have read them everything,

my prayers, and sonnets,
and Auntie Esther stories.
I would have liked to serve them
strawberry strudel in the morning,
and listened to their tales,
while washing teacups
stained in lipstick.

I should have said
I loved them,
the ladies at the reading. ✿

Close to the door

The wet night pounds
on my darkened face,
the house beautiful and soft
like a dream
one only whispers.
I imagine the living room,
bright thick rugs,
white candles burning,
fat cushioned couches,
a thousand conversations,
steam rising off blackberry cobblers.

I am afraid,
panting in my mind the way home
the way here.
Starlight only, the moon has gone
and I am cold
and feel barely seven.
I want milk and cookies,
a place on your lap.
I know I could knock,
could yell hello,
but I don't.

A black dog comes silent
from the woods,
his breath makes the same cloud
again and again.
He jumps on the porch,
presses his nose against the glass door.

And I think surely you
will look out and see us,
welcome us in.
He licks my fingers,
lazily curls into sleep
as if content and warm,
like the rain doesn't matter.

I don't want to look in the windows,
it's not polite
but that's not why I don't stare in.

The path back I know full well
from when I stopped being a child,
stopped being unborn,
the footprints once fast, confused,
now sturdy, methodical and slow.

I imagine you,
looking out into this dark place,
seeing a shadow of a woman
often leaving. ❀

Acknowledgments

In *Mennonite Life*
"Baking Bread"; 51 (4) (December 1996): 12
"Mennonite Poet"; 52 (4) (December 1997): 12-13
"At Church"; 53 (4) (December 1997) : 37-41
In *Gospel Herald*
"Heaven and Things" 90 (47) (9 December 1997): 7
In *Christian Living*
"Our Jacob Sheep" 47 (8) (December 2000): 32
In *The Mennonite*
"Martha's Story" 1 (30) (22 Sept. 1998): 11
"My People" 5 (5) (5 March 2002): 17
In *Mennonot*
"God (according to Pastor Smucker)" No. 1, Fall 1998: 15
In *Rhubarb*
"Quilt Makers" 1 (2) (Spring 1999): 30
In *Sophia*
"Mother God" 11 (1) (Spring 2001): 5
In *DreamSeeker Magazine*
"Mother God"; "Baking Bread"; "Grace," originally published as "After Church" 2 (2) (spring 2002): 2, 39.
back cover
"White Oak Park" 3 (3) (Summer 2003): back cover
In *Christian Living*
"Mother God" 49 (3) (April-May 2002): 32
In *Timbrel*
"Baby Sister" 5 (4) (July-August 2002):13
In *Pokeberry Days: A West Virginia Literary Collection.* DeBerry and Murabito, eds. Morgantown, W.V.: Goldenrod Foundation, 1995.
"Jagged Dreams" p.74

In *Wild Sweet Notes: Fifty Years of West Virginia Poetry 1950-1999.*
Barbara Smith and Kirk Judd, eds. Publishers Place, Inc.,
Huntington, WV, 2000.
"Heaven and Things" p. 96-98
"God and Farmers" p. 98-100
In *What Mennonites Are Thinking 2000.* Merle Good and Phyllis
Pellman Good, eds. Good Books, Intercourse, Pa., 2000.
"God and Farmers" p. 232-234
In *What Mennonites Are Thinking 2001.* Merle Good and Phyllis
Pellman Good, eds. Good Books: Intercourse, Pa., 2001.
"My People" p. 219-221

*A version of this poetry collection was awarded first place in the
1998 West Virginia Writers Annual Spring Competition. The
judge was Thomas E. Douglass.*

The Author

The award-winning poetry of Cheryl Denise Miller (who writes under the name Cheryl Denise) reflects vivid memories of Mennonite life in Elmira, Ontario: the red brick church, her father's print shop, the Old Order Bakery.

After nursing school Cheryl spent three years volunteering in rural Colorado where she met her husband, Mike Miller, also a service volunteer through the Mennonite Church. Cheryl's work as a public health nurse in a poor Hispanic community provided sharp contrast to sheltered early years.

Following a move to West Virginia, Cheryl continued volunteer work with Philippi Mennonite Church and the Service Adventure program, guiding young volunteers at various jobs with low income families in the county. Currently she works as a nurse at the Barbour County Senior Center coordinating in-home care services. She and her husband live on a sheep farm with the Shepherds Field community. Their life includes house building, cross-country skiing, and walks on the farm with their dog, Esau.

Printed in the United States
58771LVS00002B/37-45

9 781931 038287